ANTEATERS

Lorien Kite

Grolier
an imprint of

SCHOLASTIC

www.scholastic.com/librarypublishing

Published 2009 by Grolier
An Imprint of Scholastic Library Publishing
Old Sherman Turnpike
Danbury, Connecticut 06816

For The Brown Reference Group
Project Editor: Jolyon Goddard
Picture Researchers: Clare Newman, Sophie
Mortimer
Designer: Sarah Williams
Managing Editor: Tim Harris

Volume ISBN-13: 978-0-7172-8058-2
Volume ISBN-10: 0-7172-8058-6

**Library of Congress
Cataloging-in-Publication Data**

Nature's children. Set 6.
    p. cm.
  Includes index.
  ISBN-13: 978-0-7172-8085-8
  ISBN-10: 0-7172-8085-3
  1. Animals--Encyclopedias, Juvenile. 1.
Grolier (Firm)
  QL49.N387 2009
  590.3--dc22
                              2008014675

Printed and bound in China

PICTURE CREDITS

Front Cover: **Shutterstock**: Nestor Noci.

Back Cover: **NHPA**: Haroldo Palo Jr.;
Shutterstock: Karel Gallas, Michael Ledray,
Alexey Stiop.

Corbis: Tom Brakefield 5, 6, 17, 18, 29; Joel
Creed 9, 10, Peter Johnson 25, Joe McDonald
13, 33, Darren Maybury 22, Richard Hamilton
Smith 30; **NHPA**: Daniel Heuclin 14, Haroldo
Palo Jr. 21, 37, 40–41, Jany Sauvanet 26, 42,
45, 46, George Lepp 2–3, 34; **Photos.com** 4.

Contents

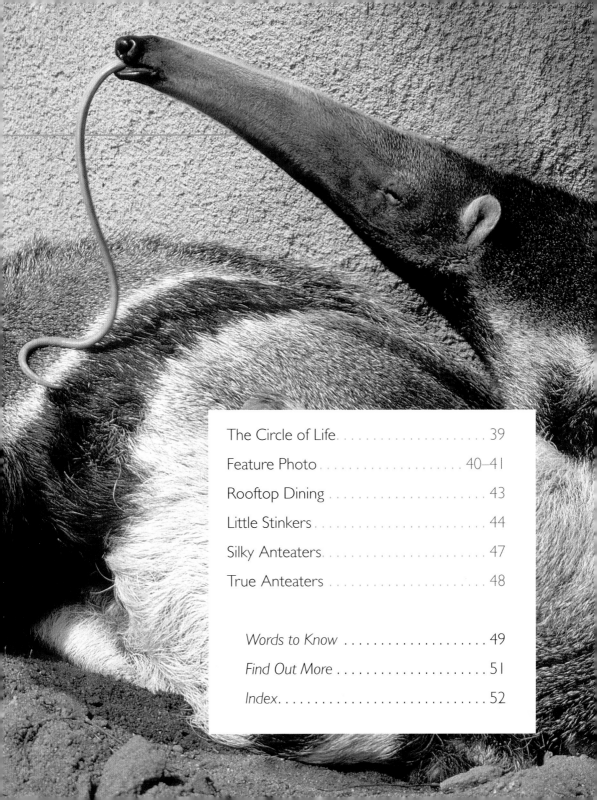

FACT FILE: Giant Anteaters

Class	Mammals (Mammalia)
Order	Anteaters (Pilosa)
Family	Giant anteaters and tamanduas (Myrmecophagidae)
Genus	*Myrmecophaga*
Species	Giant anteater (*Myrmecophaga tridactyla*)
World distribution	South and Central America
Habitat	Savannas, forests, and swamplands
Distinctive physical characteristics	Narrow, tubelike snout; extremely long, wormlike tongue; large, curved claws; mainly gray-brown in color; large, bulky tail; coarse coat of hair, very long on the back and tail
Habits	Solitary and territorial; defend themselves ferociously when attacked; active mainly during the day; young are born singly and carried on their mother's back; communicate by scent marking; generally silent; strong swimmers
Diet	Ants and termites

Introduction

Anteaters are some of the pickiest eaters. They pretty much eat only ants and termites—also known as white ants. There are just four types, or **species**, of true anteaters. The best known is the ground-dwelling giant anteater. The northern tamandua and the southern tamandua, spend time both on the ground and in trees. The smallest type of anteater is the silky anteater. It lives almost exclusively in trees.

The giant anteater is by far the biggest type of true anteater. True anteaters are also known as hairy anteaters.

5

Wandering across the savanna, the shy and solitary giant anteater is rarely seen by people.

Savanna Giant

Imagine yourself alone on a South American **savanna**. An endless sea of swaying grass, sparsely scattered with thorn bushes and small trees, stretches to the horizon.

In the distance, you see a dark shape moving slowly through the tall grasses. Its body and enormous tail are covered with coarse gray-brown hair. Black diagonal stripes run up each side of its back. Holding its narrow, tubelike **snout** close to the ground, it stops once every few steps to tap the earth with a long, curved **claw**.

This is the giant anteater, searching for insects in the sunbaked earth. It may look strange to you—but this shy, solitary creature is perfectly suited for the life it leads.

Many Habitats

There are four types, or species, of anteaters. The largest is the giant anteater. From the tip of its snout to the end of its tail, this creature can grow as long as 7 feet (2.1 m).

Giant anteaters live in a variety of **habitats**, including swamplands, **rain forests**, and dry woodlands. Their favorite places, however, are the vast, open savannas that lie both north and south of the great **Amazon rain forest**.

Found in tropical parts of the world, savannas are hot, grassy plains with few trees. For a few months each year it rains heavily, but for the rest of the time it is very dry. Savannas are very rich in wildlife. Many have been made into large nature **reserves**.

The savannas of South America often become flooded during the brief rainy season.

Baked by the sun, the earth walls of a termites' mound become as hard as rock, protecting the insects inside.

Huge Meals

When they are not sleeping, giant anteaters spend almost all of their time searching for food. They need to eat at least 30,000 ants and termites every day! Fortunately for the anteaters, these tiny insects live together in huge, well-organized groups. Despite their small size, termites can be caught in large numbers at one time to provide a decent meal.

Termites live in large mounds that they build by chewing up earth and mixing it with their own **saliva**. The combination of earth and saliva makes a kind of liquid cement. Termites' mounds can stand 12 feet (4 m) tall and may contain many millions of insects.

Giant anteaters prefer to eat types of ants that build their nests underground. Although they are less obvious than termites' mounds, underground ants' nests can be even bigger, covering areas the size of football fields.

Strong Sniffers

Ants and termites rarely leave their nests.
Protected by fierce guards, the **queen** remains
deep inside the nest throughout her life, laying
eggs that will hatch into new members of the
colony. Her **workers** occasionally venture out
to collect food. However, even the workers
spend most of their time hidden away, traveling
through a vast network of covered feeding trails.

Giant anteaters hardly seem equipped to
track down these cautious insects. Their hearing
is poor, and their vision is even worse. A person
could probably creep within 30 feet (10 m) of
one before it noticed anyone was there.

What anteaters do have, however, is an
extremely powerful sense of smell. By holding
their sensitive snout close to the ground, giant
anteaters are able to sniff out insect colonies
with pinpoint accuracy.

A giant anteater concentrates on sniffing out some ants.

A giant anteater walks on its knuckles, keeping its long claws tucked away to stop them from being worn down by the hard ground.

Claws of Life

It is not easy to break through the sunbaked earth of the savanna, and even harder to get into a termites' mound. Without a sharp spade or a pickax, most people would find it impossible.

The giant anteater's 4-to-6-inch (10-to-15-cm) front claws enable it to break into ants' nests and termites' mounds with ease. To keep its claws razor sharp, the anteater scratches at trees whenever it gets the chance.

One of the claws on a giant anteater's front foot is much bigger than the others. The anteater uses this powerful claw to make the initial break into the termites' mound. All the anteater's strength is concentrated into the big claw's sharp point as the animal attempts to break through the mound's tough walls. This concentration of strength into a point works in much the same way as when a person pushes a thumbtack into a wall.

Talented Tongue

When a giant anteater locates its meal, it carefully makes a few holes in the earth with its long claw. Then, after widening the hole with a few circular movements of the snout, it flicks its tongue deep into the nest, throwing the insects into confusion.

A giant anteater's tongue is truly amazing. Longer than most humans' arms, an anteater's tongue can thrust about 22 inches (55 cm) into a nest, darting in and out of the animal's mouth at a rate of 160 strokes per minute. On each return journey, tiny inward-pointing spikes on the tongue sweep the insects out of their nest and into the anteater's stomach.

An anteater covers its tongue in thick, sticky saliva. This turns the tongue into a natural flypaper, ideal for collecting small insects.

After breaking
into a rotting log,
a giant anteater
feeds on the ants
that have made
their nest inside.

Meals on the Go!

Giant anteaters never chew their food. In fact, they have no teeth to chew with! To make up for that, they have an extremely muscular stomach that can grind up food before they **digest** it. The earth and gravel that anteaters swallow by accident also help crush up the insects in their stomach.

One advantage of eating this way is that it is very fast. Giant anteaters need to eat as quickly as possible. Each of their meals is a race against time. Why do they have to eat fast? The anteater's **prey** are not as helpless as their small size might suggest!

Insect Armies

Just like humans, many ant and termite species have armies of **soldiers**. The armies rush to defend their homes as soon as they realize that they are being attacked. Like human soldiers, they are specially armed for their role. They have large pincers, or **mandibles**, which they use to bite intruders. Another similarity between ant and human soldiers is that, when all else fails, both are prepared to sacrifice their life in a desperate attempt to ward off the enemy. Bravely, they launch themselves at the anteater, swarming up its nose and biting it on its tongue hard.

By the time the soldiers arrive on the scene, hundreds of insects will have already perished. Once the biting starts, however, the anteater soon moves on to find another nest or mound. The insects can then rebuild their home.

A queen termite surrounded by her guards and workers. The guards are slightly bigger than the workers and have large pincers on their head.

An ant soldier ready to attack. Anteaters try to avoid the most poisonous species of ants.

Venomous Ants

As if biting weren't bad enough on its own, many ant species have poisons in their bodies and can inject **venom** with their pincers. If an anteater were to dine on only one type of ant, it might get sick as a result of eating too much of that type of ant's venom. To cope with that, anteaters range far and wide when they hunt. There are thousands of species of ants. Frequently moving allows the anteater to make sure that it eats many different types of ants in the course of a day. By feeding in this way, many poisons from different ant species can be absorbed in small, harmless quantities.

Not all ants bite or poison their attackers. Some just run away. In the savanna, their nests are often so big that they can eventually outdistance the giant anteater's searching tongue.

Year After Year

Anteaters are **territorial** animals. Day after day, year after year, they walk the same paths, often going back to trusted spots where they know they can get a good meal. Fortunately for the anteater, their prey are very difficult to catch. If an anteater were to wipe out all the ants in its territory, it would have to move somewhere else.

If you were to follow an anteater and inspect the places where it has fed, you would hardly notice any damage. Anteaters are not pointlessly destructive. In fact, they are careful not to damage nests and mounds beyond the point of repair. In a way, anteaters are like farmers, carefully managing their resources so that they last a lifetime and beyond.

Worker and guard termites quickly move in to repair the damage to their home.

On its own patch an anteater definitely prefers to be left alone.

No Trespassing

An anteater patrols a territory of up to 9 square miles (23 sq km). Although its territory usually overlaps slightly at the edges with the territories of other anteaters, meetings between these solitary creatures are extremely rare. If two meet on shared land, they usually just ignore each other and wander off in opposite directions.

When a stranger strays too far into its territory, however, an anteater will circle the intruder menacingly. If the trespasser doesn't leave immediately, the anteater whose territory it is will start pushing or even slashing at the unwelcome guest with its claws. Such fights can occasionally lead to serious injuries.

Humans are the greatest threat to giant anteaters. The destruction of the anteaters' savannas has forced the animals to live in an increasingly small area. As a result, fighting and starvation have reduced their numbers to dangerous levels.

Fierce Fighters

Giant anteaters have few natural **predators**. Their huge tail and bushy coat make them look even bigger than they are, so they are only rarely attacked by the cougars and jaguars that share their habitat. Giant anteaters are careful, too, and gallop off at the slightest hint of trouble. The big cats, however, are faster runners, and sometimes an anteater will have to stay and fight.

Although it only ever fights in self-defense, the giant anteater is a tough opponent. Using its tail to help it balance, a cornered anteater will rear up on its hind legs and draw back its muscular forearms. Then, falling forward, it will fling its arms around the enemy, stabbing it with its huge claws.

Big cats do not usually dare to attack giant anteaters. They could easily end up severely injured—or at worst, dead.

Even jaguars, the largest cats in South America, only attack giant anteaters when desperate for food.

29

Fire spreads quickly
through the dry
grass of the savanna.
Anteaters must be
alert to stay out
of trouble.

Floods and Fires

Each year, when the rains come, many of the rivers that flow through the great plains of northern Brazil and Venezuela burst their banks, causing huge floods. Luckily, giant anteaters are strong swimmers. Even in the dry season, they often cross large rivers in the course of their daily wanderings.

With much of the savanna underwater, however, it becomes harder for anteaters to find their favorite types of ants. They are forced to eat more termites, which, safe in their mounds, are able to survive the floods.

Even so, the rainy season is a welcomed time of year. By the end of the long dry season, the land is so parched that fires can start easily and spread quickly through the savanna. The anteaters must avoid the flames at all costs. Their coat of long, coarse hair can catch fire easily.

Day and Night

Giant anteaters sleep for about 14 hours each day. They often take short naps after a meal to sleep off the effects of any poisons in their food. In isolated, safe areas they also like to sleep throughout the night. Giant anteaters that live near towns or villages, however, often travel only under the cover of darkness. Those anteaters sleep through the daylight hours to avoid any contact with humans.

Giant anteaters are not that picky about where they sleep. Sometimes they shelter in abandoned **burrows** or hollow logs, but usually they just find a sheltered ditch and bed down under the stars. For protection from the sun, rain, or cold, they tuck their long snout between their forelegs and cover their body with their huge tail. A sleeping anteater could easily be mistaken for a bush!

With its nose between its paws, a giant anteater rests in the sunshine.

33

Two giant anteaters play
and rest together in a zoo.

Getting Together

In most areas, the **mating season** of giant anteaters runs from March to May, although matings can occur throughout the year. Though normally unsociable creatures, anteaters do not have trouble finding mates. When the time is right, a female giant anteater gives off an extremely strong scent. Sooner or later, a nearby male picks up this scent and tracks the female down. To show his interest, he touches her gently with his paw and lays his head on her back. The two anteaters then spend the rest of the day play-fighting and getting to know each other.

After mating, the two go their separate ways, never to meet again. Six months later a single baby is born.

First Days

As soon as a giant anteater is born, it climbs up onto its mother's back and buries its head in her coat. That is where it will spend most of the next six months.

It is only when a giant anteater is seen with her baby that the purpose of her black diagonal stripes becomes clear. While in piggyback position, the baby's stripe finishes off its mother's. With its tiny head buried in her coat, it blends in perfectly, and the two look like one animal. So what passing cougars and jaguars see is not a small and vulnerable meal, but one particularly large anteater—not to be interfered with!

The baby anteater drinks its mother's milk for several months. Toward the end of this nursing period, the baby becomes interested in ants. It scampers up close when its mother breaks into a nest and slurps up any ants that wander its way.

Hidden in its mother's furry coat, a baby giant anteater is safe from predators.

Big Baby!

A young anteater is a playful creature. Unfortunately, it has no one to play with except its mother! It loves dancing around her and challenging her with mock attacks. Tolerant and protective, the mother usually responds by laying her head on the youngster's back—her way of saying, "Calm down!"

At about six months old, a giant anteater begins to make short, careful trips away from its mother to explore its surroundings. At the first sign of trouble, however, it scampers back onto the safety of its mother's back. Even after nine months, when it is almost as big as its mother, it still tries to jump on. At this point, however, the mother does her best to dodge her big baby. Weighing 65 pounds (30 kg), the young anteater is much too heavy for her to carry around.

The Circle of Life

At about one year old, a giant anteater is fully grown. However, it will need another six months or so to reach its full weight of about 120 pounds (55 kg). Its mother has taught it how to survive on its own, but there are not enough ants in her territory to support them both. At this time, the young anteater leaves its mother to find its own territory. It may have to travel a long way before finding the perfect spot, and it will almost certainly never see her again.

Throughout its life, the giant anteater will face danger from big cats, other anteaters, fires, floods, and most of all, humans. After about three or four years, it will be able to have young of its own. If it is very lucky, it will wander the plains for its full life span of about 25 years—by which time it will have eaten more than 200 million ants!

Giant anteaters are not
the only animals that
walk on their knuckles.
Gorillas, chimpanzees,
and platypuses walk
in this way, too.

A tamandua grips a tree trunk with its strong tail. That helps it climb down safely.

Rooftop Dining

Tropical rain forests crawl with insects. There, ants and termites build their nests high up in the trees, way out of the giant anteater's reach. Getting at these insects is no problem for the other types of anteaters, though. Both types of tamanduas and the silky anteater are perfectly at home in the trees.

A tamandua is about the size of a cat. Unlike the giant anteater, the tamandua can use its tail to grasp hold of branches when it climbs. That gives it extra security in the trees.

As well as a grasping tail, the squirrel-sized silky anteater has large pads on its forepaws and feet, which form natural grooves for thin branches to fit among. The silky anteater's grip is so strong that even when it loses its balance it can still hold on, hanging upside down.

Little Stinkers

In proportion to their body, tamanduas have a shorter snout than giant anteaters. However, their ears and eyes are larger. Their coloring varies from blond to dark brown. Tamanduas from central and southern parts of South America also have black "vests" on their coat.

Tamanduas look clumsy on land and are not able to gallop. Still, there are many living in savannas and croplands. They are by far the most common kind of anteater.

To mark their territory, tamanduas produce a foul smelling liquid that lingers on everything they touch. The Guarani (GWAR-UH-NEE) tribe of the Amazon rain forest hates it so much that their name for the tamandua is *caguaré*, which means "forest stinker."

Like giant anteaters, tamanduas rear up on their back legs and show their claws when threatened.

The common, but rarely seen, silky anteater feeds on beetles and fruits in addition to ants and termites.

Silky Anteaters

The silky anteater gets its name from the silvery or golden yellow color of its smooth coat. It is completely **nocturnal** and never comes down to the ground.

Because of their small size, silky anteaters are particularly vulnerable to enemies such as snakes and prowling wildcats. They spend most of their time on thin branches, where these predators cannot reach them. Even there, they are not completely safe. They may be carried off by swooping eagles, owls, and hawks.

Perhaps because of the danger from above, silky anteaters spend most of their time in the kapok, or silk-cotton tree. That tree is covered with soft, silvery seed pods. Side by side, a silky anteater and a seed pod look almost identical, especially at night. The anteater, therefore, is usually not seen by passing predators.

True Anteaters

There are animals in Africa, Asia, and Australia that, at first glance, look very similar to the South American anteaters. Aardvarks, pangolins, and spiny anteaters all have a long snout, a wormlike tongue, and powerful claws—these animals also feed on insects.

Scientists used to think that all these animals were related to one another. They classed them as **edentates** (EE-DEN-TAITS), which means "animals without teeth." Eventually, scientists discovered that aardvarks, pangolins, and spiny anteaters do in fact have small, barely noticeable teeth. Hairy anteaters are the only members of the group with no teeth at all.

Scientists now know that none of these animals are closely related. They only look similar because they all specialize in eating insects. Because of this confusion hairy anteaters are also called "true" anteaters.

Words to Know

Amazon rain forest	The largest rain forest in the world, covering most of central and northern Brazil.
Burrows	Homes dug by animals.
Claw	A nail, often long and sharp, at the end of an animal's toe.
Colony	A large group of animals that lives together.
Digest	To break down food in the body.
Edentates	Mammals with few or no teeth, including anteaters, armadillos, and sloths.
Habitats	Types of places in which animals and plants naturally live.
Mandibles	The pincer mouthparts of insects.
Mating season	The time of the year when animals come together to produce young.
Nocturnal	Active only at night.
Predators	Animals that hunt other animals.
Prey	An animal hunted by other animals.

Queen	The ruler of a colony of insects. The queen lays eggs that hatch into new workers and guards.
Rain forests	Dense tropical forests in areas of high rainfall.
Reserves	Areas where plants and animals are protected.
Saliva	A fluid produced in the mouth of animals to help digest food.
Savanna	A grassy plain with few trees.
Snout	The nose and jaws of an animal.
Soldiers	Ants and termites that protect their nest from intruders.
Species	The scientific word for animals of the same kind that breed together.
Territorial	Describing an animal that defends its own private space.
Venom	A harmful chemical injected through a bite or sting.
Workers	Insects in a colony that perform the day-to-day duties, such as finding food and maintaining the nest.

Find Out More

Books

Rebman, R. C. *Anteaters*. Animals Animals. New York: Benchmark Books, 2007.

Seiple, T., and S. Seiple. *Giant Anteaters*. Early Bird Nature Books. Minneapolis, Minnesota: Lerner Publications, 2007.

Web sites

Anteaters
www.enchantedlearning.com/subjects/mammals/anteater/Anteaterprintout.shtml
Facts about anteaters and a diagram to print.

Giant Anteater
animals.nationalgeographic.com/animals/mammals/giant-anteater.html
A profile of the giant anteater.

Index